Landry Mate Gilgen

DESIGN AND IMPLEMENTATION OF A DATABASE

Landry Mate Gilgen

DESIGN AND IMPLEMENTATION OF A DATABASE

By an explicit classical method approach based on the merise method with verification of the result

ScienciaScripts

Imprint

Any brand names and product names mentioned in this book are subject to trademark, brand or patent protection and are trademarks or registered trademarks of their respective holders. The use of brand names, product names, common names, trade names, product descriptions etc. even without a particular marking in this work is in no way to be construed to mean that such names may be regarded as unrestricted in respect of trademark and brand protection legislation and could thus be used by anyone.

Cover image: www.ingimage.com

This book is a translation from the original published under ISBN 978-620-2-26263-7.

Publisher:
Sciencia Scripts
is a trademark of
Dodo Books Indian Ocean Ltd. and OmniScriptum S.R.L publishing group

120 High Road, East Finchley, London, N2 9ED, United Kingdom
Str. Armeneasca 28/1, office 1, Chisinau MD-2012, Republic of Moldova, Europe
Printed at: see last page
ISBN: 978-620-5-78072-5

Contents

FOREWORD

Currently, the world is experiencing a considerable technological advance in all sectors thanks to computer science, which is a science that studies the techniques of automatic information processing. It plays an important role in the development of business and other institutions.

Before the invention of the computer, all information was recorded manually on paper, which caused many problems such as loss of time in searching for the information, damage to the information, etc.

Thus, up to now, the computer remains the most reliable means of processing and storing information. This invention has made it possible to computerise the data systems of companies, which is the essential part in their development today.

SUMMARY

This book aims to shed light on the implementation of normalized transactional databases in a rigorous manner. By presenting the steps of the implementation according to the approach proposed by the method of study and computer implementation of evolved systems. This is an R&D approach intended for professionals and researchers in computer science wishing to set up databases respecting the standards (FN). This approach starts with the identification of the needs of the end-users of the database, continues with a systematic application of the steps of the approach proposed by the MERISE method and ends with an implementation of the database with a verification of the expected results of the database via SQL queries.

This research also shows that common sense (the designer's judgement) remains essential in the application of the rules of passage and standardisation.

GENERAL INTRODUCTION

They appeared many years ago and are not about to disappear. They are becoming ubiquitous, and in all areas.

They are used to store exponentially increasing volumes of data, their uses are becoming more and more varied, as are the tools used to exploit them. All types of data are being stored, from user information, to images, to mapping information, to morphing for facial recognition. The rapid evolution of the web and mobile applications is generating quantities of new data, and has led to a need for very simple and easy to implement storage engines. All this information is not only stored, but processed to obtain indicators and trends, which is where BI and Big Data come in. It is a market that is evolving very quickly and the players sometimes find it difficult to keep up. (Nicolas Moreau, 2017).

These statements demonstrate not only the omnipresence, but also and above all the relevance of databases in the daily lives of both companies and households. Also, decision support depends on transactional databases (transactional databases serve as a feeder for decisional databases)

The lack of rigour in setting up transactional databases accentuates the difficulties of designing decisional databases. Hence the need for a systematic pedagogy in the design of transactional databases. The choice of database development approach is therefore a step to be taken very seriously.

When using a **"classical"** approach, the project, its functionality and purpose are clearly defined in advance. This method is based on the use of a strict process, the drafting of detailed documentation and less involvement of the client. It consists of defining all the project's functionalities, specifying them in detail, developing them and then testing them before validation and commissioning. This approach is more appropriate for database design as the needs of the end users are known in advance. What can be done with the data is known in advance, and the designer can even anticipate future needs for the database, provided that the context of the study is well defined.

CHAPTER 1

PROBLEMATICS

Developing an application with an **agile** method is very different. Using an agile method involves a lighter methodology, smaller tasks, fast delivery of increments and constant communication between the client and the development team. The key word is flexibility, both in terms of planning and incremental functionality.

Flexibility in the design of a database implies that the designer does not master all user needs beforehand and increases the risk of ending up with a database full of inconsistencies and undesirable redundancies. This is because the evolutionary (iterative and incremental) life cycle model, from a technical point of view, exposes various risks such as (Musangu Luka, 2020).

- Invisibility of the development process: managers need to make regular deliveries to measure progress. If systems are developed rapidly, it is difficult to produce documents that reflect all versions of the system.

- Poor database structuring: continuous change tends to corrupt the structure of software modules. Integrating the various software changes is becoming increasingly difficult and costly.

- Special tools and techniques may be needed: These facilitate rapid development, but they may be incompatible with other tools or techniques and relatively few people may have the skills to use them.

- In the light of the above, a fundamental question arises: How do we go about setting up a standardised database that meets all the needs of its end users?

CHAPTER 2

GENERAL CONCEPTS ON THE DATA BASE

A database is a set of data that models objects in a part of the real world and supports a computer application. To merit the term database, a set of non-independent data must be searchable by content. The data must be searchable by any criteria. It must be possible to retrieve their structure [1]

A Database Management System (DBMS), on the other hand, can be thought of as a set of system software that allows users to efficiently insert, modify and search for specific data in a large body of information shared by multiple users. The information is stored on secondary memories, usually magnetic disks. Searches can be performed based on the value of a data item designated by a name in a set, but also based on relationships between objects [GARD 03, p. 3]. Among the database management software we can mention: Oracle, Ingres, SQL Server, DB2, Access, My SQL, PostGre...

Databases are currently at the heart of the information system of companies. They have taken an important place in computer science, and particularly in management.

---

[1] L. HAINAUT. Bases de données et modèles de calcul, Dunod, Paris, 2000. [GARD 03] G. GARDARIN. Bases de données, Eyrolles, Paris, 2003.

CHAPTER 3

METHODOLOGICAL APPROACH

The design of an information system is not obvious, because one has to think about the whole organisation that is to be put in place. The design phase requires methods to establish a model (a description) on which to build. Modelling consists of creating a virtual representation of a reality in such a way as to bring out the points of interest. This type of method is called analysis [DIGA 01, p.5].

It is also difficult to model a domain in a form directly usable by a DBMS. One or more intermediate models are therefore useful, the entity-association model being one of the first and most common. This model allows a natural description of the real world from the concepts of entity and association. Based on the theory of sets and relations, this model is intended to be universal and meets the objective of data-program independence. This model, used for the design phase, is part of a more general and widespread method, called MERISE, which we use in this study.

MERISE is an acronym that stands for Method d'Etudes et de Realisations Informatiques par Sous-Ensemble. The MERISE method separates data and processing. This method is perfectly adapted to the modelling of problems approached from a functional point of view. The data represents the static of the information system and the processes its dynamic. MERISE proposes an approach by levels. These levels of modelling are organised in a double approach data - processing

1. PRESENTATION OF THE PROCEDURE

a.   **Example of a problem to solve**

A transport company wishes to computerise the management of its activities. Indeed, we wish to have a system that will allow :

-    To manage all the drivers that we recruit (assignment of the personnel manager).

-    Analyse the   proximity of a   candidate 's place of   residence driver in   relation to the location of the company, question to avoid lateness at work (assigned by the Head of Personnel).

-    To manage the   situation of   the pay situation of the drivers, it should be noted that a driveris paid at the   end of eachat the end of each month at the rate of 12% of the the total of its payments, the value of which is determined by the employer (cashier's allocation).

-    To manage the cars (each driver has a car at his disposal, no one else drives it in his absence, unless there is a special permission from the employer). Each car has a well-defined route (changing the route is also possible with a special permission of the employer) (assignment of the head of the motor transport).

-    Plan car maintenance (allocation of the head of personnel);

-    Identify recurring breakdowns for each make of vehicle to guide car maintenance (allocation by the Head of Personnel).

When there is a recruitment advertisement, the candidates each come and fill in an identification form where they fill in their identities. Then comes the recruitment test which determines whether a candidate is selected or not. When a candidate is selected, he completes his file by adding the contact details of at least one trusted person to be contacted in case of problems, before signing his contract which also gives information on the car that the new driver will drive in this company.

The driver will follow the route marked on his car every day, unless he has a special authorisation to go elsewhere, and will pay a fixed sum of money to the cashier at the end of each day. After a certain period of time (usually depending on the number of days the car is out), or in case of a breakdown, the car goes to the garage for maintenance or repair.

At the end of each month, a report must come from the cashier after the drivers have been paid and another report must come from the garage on the maintenance and repairs carried out during the month.

This statement more or less spells out the needs of the end users of the database.

b.   **Application of MERISE principles**

1)   Implementation of the conceptual data model

The MCD is the best known element of MERISE and certainly the most useful. It allows to establish a clear representation of the data of the IS and defines the functional dependencies of these data between them. The steps for the construction of this model are :

Step 1: Identification of entities

After reading the statement, we have identified the following objects:

- Candidate ;

- Driver ;

- Payroll ;

- Payment ;

- Car ;

- Failure ;

- Itinerary ;

- Interview;

- Repair ;

- Test ;

- Contract ;

- Trusted person.

Step 2: Description of the entities

N°	Entities/Objects	Properties	Mnemonic	Identifier
1	Candidate	Applicant number	Num_cdt	#
		Name	Name_cdt	
		Postname	Pstnom_cdt	
		First name	Prnom_cdt	
		Gender	Gender	
		Date of birth	Date_naiss	
		Address	Adr_cdt	
2	Driver	Driver's registration number	Matr_chf	#
		Name	Name_chf	
		Postname	Pstnom_chf	
		First name	Prnom_chf	
		Gender	Gender	
		Date of birth	Date_naiss	
		Telephone	Tel	
		Address	Adr_chf	
3	Payroll	Payroll number	Num_py	#
		Description	Description	
		Observation	Observation	
4	Payment	Payment number	Num_vrst	#
		Observation	Observation	
		Amount		
5	Car	Car number	Matr_vtr	#
		Description	Description	
		Brand	Brand	
6	Itinerary	Route code	Inr_code	#
		Description	Description	
7	Maintenance	Maintenance code	Code_entt	#
		Observation	Observation	
8	Test	Test ID	Id_tst	#
		Observation	Observation	
9	Person_of_trust	Person's ID	Id_pers	#
		Name	Name	

		First name	First name	
		Telephone	Tel_ref	
10	Contract	Contract number	Num_Ctr	#
		Description	Description	
		Observation	Observation	
11	Breakdown	Fault number	Num_pn	#
		Description	Description	
12	Repair	Repair number	Num_rep	#
		Observation	Observation	

Step 3: Identification of relationships

After reading the statement, we have identified the following relationships:

N°	Relationship	Associated objects	Nature	Observation
1	Go to	Candidate and Test	Binary	There is a date to take the test, each time the test is taken, there will be a result. Hence the relationship will have two properties: Date and result.
2	Become	Applicant and Driver	Binary	Drivers are recruited from among the applicants. So some candidates become effective drivers.
3	Drive	Driver and Car	Binary	Each driver drives a car. Since on special permission a driver can drive another car, it is desirable to know when a driver X drove a car Y. Hence the date as a property of the relationship in addition to the description of the permission.
4	Touch	Driver and Payroll	Binary	At the end of each month, each driver gets paid. The end of the month also represents a date. So we can have a date property for the relationship Touch, but also and especially the amount touched.
5	Carry out	Driver and Payment	Binary	At the end of each working day, the driver makes a payment to the cashier. A day of work represents a given date, hence the date property for the Perform relationship, as well as the amount paid.
6	Associate	Car and Route	Binary	A route is written on each car, but one can change the route (associate the car with a new route) with special permission. So for the Associate relationship, there are properties: Number of the permission, date of the permission etc.
7	Fill in	Driver and	Binary	Each driver provides the contact

		Person of Confidence		details of at least one contact person.
8	Sign	Driver and Contract	Binary	Each driver signs an employment contract. The contract is signed on a specific date. Hence the date ownership for the relationship Sign
9	Go to	Car and Maintenance	Binary	After a well-defined period, each The car goes in for maintenance. The determination of the service date depends on the date of the previous service. Done we will have a property date for the relationship Know.
10	Get to know	Car and breakdown	Binary	A car can break down on a given date. Hence the date property for the relationship
11	Submit	Car and Repair	Binary	A car goes for repairs when it breaks down. The date on which the car was repaired can be used as the property of the relationship.
12	Concerning	Repair and Breakdown	Binary	A repair concerns a breakdown.

Step 4: Determination of cardinalities

N°	Relationship	Associated objects	Nature	Cardinalite Source	ICF	Target cardinalite
1	Go to	Candidate and Test	Binary	1, n	yes	1, n
2	Become	Applicant and Driver	Binary	1,1	not	1,1
3	Drive	Driver and Car	Binary	1, n	yes	1, n
4	Touch	Driver and Payroll	Binary	1, n	yes	1, n
5	Carry out	Driver and Payment	Binary	1, n	yes	1, 1
6	Associate	Car and Route	Binary	1, n	yes	1, n
7	Fill in	Driver and Trusted Person	Binary	1, n	yes	1, n
8	Sign	Driver and Contract	Binary	1, 1	not	1, 1
9	Go to	Car and Maintenance	Binary	1, n	yes	1, 1
10	Get to know	Car and breakdown	Binary	1, n	yes	1, n
11	Submit	Car and Repair	Binary	1, n	yes	1, 1
12	Concerning	Repair and Breakdown	Binary	1, 1	yes	1, n

Step 5: Presentation of the Conceptual Donwes Model

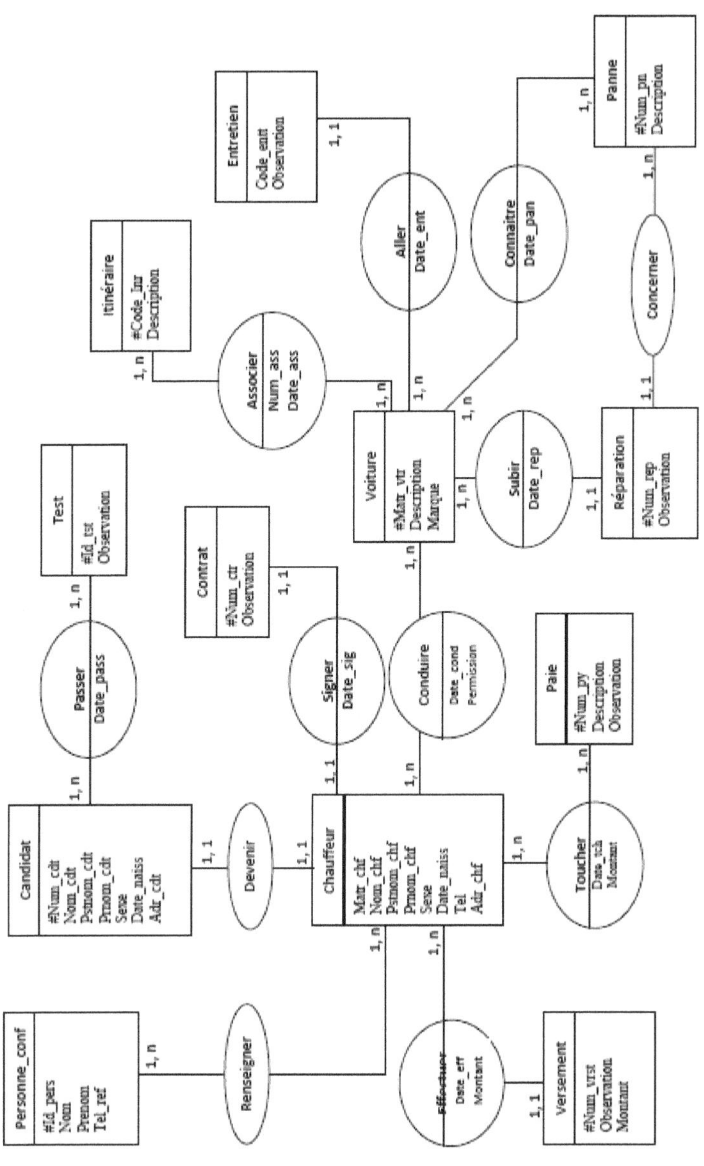

2) Implementation of the Organisational Data Model

Step 1: Choice of data to be stored electronically (Production of the Global MOD)

The data identified so far are data that make up the MCD. The aim here is to analyse the importance of each entity and to decide on its existence in the following. This choice involves the following question: *Do we manage the data of these entities, or are they only there to complete or reinforce the precision of the data of the more important entities that we really want to manage?*

In order to make the right choice of data to be stored, it is necessary to keep an eye on the users' needs (see problem statement). Thus we summarize the decisions in the following table:

N°	Entity	Decision	Observation
1	Candidate	Withheld	To analyse the proximity of the place of residence before recruitment
2	Driver	Withheld	To manage drivers
3	Test	Not retained	No user needs depend on this entity. There is no need to keep the data related to the test in the database.
4	Payroll	Withheld	To manage the drivers' payroll.
5	Payment	Withheld	For calculate the salary of driver
6	Car	Withheld	To manage the cars.
7	Itinerary	Withheld	For know itinerary each vehicle.
8	Maintenance	Withheld	For plan the next interviews.
9	Repair	Withheld	For the garage report.
10	Trusted_person	Not retained	This information can be considered as property of the driver entity, without any problems in the following.
11	Contract	Not retained	We can just keep the number and type of contract as properties of the driver entity, without it having problems in the following.
12	Breakdown	Not retained	To identify failures and plan interviews, yes. But you can directly integratepanne as property of the object Repair without distorting the logic of things. That is to say, each

		time a car is repaired, the relevant breakdowns are registered at the same time.

Hence the following **global MOD**:

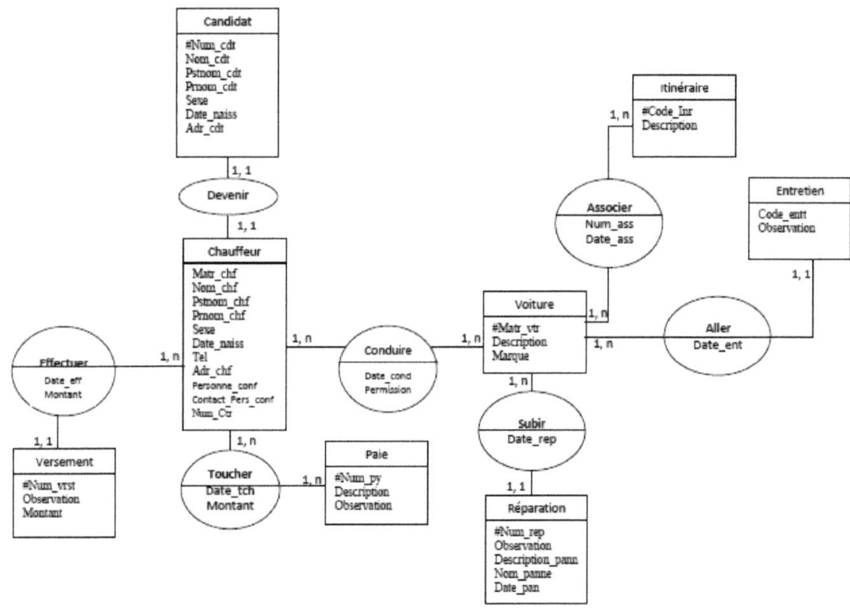

Candidat
#Num_cdt
Nom_cdt
Pstnom_cdt
Prnom_cdt
Sexe
Date_naiss
Adr_cdt

1, 1
Devenir
1, 1

Chauffeur
Matr_chf
Nom_chf
Pstnom_chf
Prnom_chf
Sexe
Date_naiss
Tel
Adr_chf
Personne_conf
Contact_Pers_conf
Num_Ctr

Effectuer
Date_eff
Montant
1, n

1, 1
Versement
#Num_vrst
Observation
Montant

1, n
Conduire
Date_cond
Permission

1, n
Toucher
Date_tch
Montant

1, n
Paie
#Num_py
Description
Observation

Itinéraire
#Code_Inr
Description
1, n

Associer
Num_ass
Date_ass

Voiture
#Matr_vtr
Description
Marque
1, n

1, n

Entretien
Code_entt
Observation
1, 1

Aller
Date_ent
1, n

1, n
Subir
Date_rep
1, 1

Réparation
#Num_rep
Observation
Description_pann
Nom_panne
Date_pan

Step 2: Estimating the useful volume for the database

a. Quantification of objects

We will estimate the size of each <u>entity (estimated size for a complete record)</u> in number of characters (bytes).

N°	Entities/Objects	Properties	Size in Byte (Ta)	Object size (STa)	Estimated number of occurrences (Ne)	Volume of the object ((STa)*Ne)
1	Candidate	Num cdt	4	120	19250	2310000
		Name	20			
		Pstnom cdt	20			
		Prnom cdt	20			
		Gender	1			
		Date of birth	10			
		Adr cdt	45			
2	Driver	Matr chf	5	192	2500	480000
		Name chf	20			
		Pstnom chf	20			
		Prnom chf	20			
		Gender	1			
		Date of birth	10			
		Tel	13			
		Adr chf	45			
		No one confided	40			
		Contact Pers conf	13			
		Num Ctr	5			
3	Payroll	Num py	4	54	65000	3510000
		Description	25			
		Observation	25			
4	Payment	Num vrst	6	31	265000	8215000
		Observation	25			
5	Car	Matr vtr	8	168	250	42000
		Description	25			
		Brand	15			
		Model	20			

		Observation	50			
		Other	50			
6	Itinerary	Inr code	3	28	100	2800
		Description	25			
7	Maintenance	Code entt	5	55	65000	3575000
		Observation	50			
8	Repair	Rep Num	5	140	10000	1400000
		Description pann	50			
		Name pan	40			
		Observation	45			

^ object volume = 19534800(1)

b. Quantification of relationships

N°	Relationship	Properties	Size in Byte	Size of the relationship	Number of occurrences Of the relationship	Volume of the relationship
1	Become	-	0	0	0	0
2	Carry out	Date_eff	10	10	0	0
		Amount	10	10		
3	Touch	Date_Tch	10	16	10000	160000
		Amount	6			
4	Drive	Date_cond	10	60	2000	120000
		Permission	50			
5	Associate	Num_ass	4	14	1500	21000
		Date_ass	10			
6	Go to	Date_entr	10	10	0	0
7	Submit	Date_rep	10	10	0	0

$^\wedge$volume relationship = 301000 (2)

c.   Calculation of the useful volume

Useful volume = (S object volume + S relation volume) x safety coefficient

= ((1) + (2)) x safety coefficient

= (19534800 + 301000) x 3

= 5950007400 bytes

-        58113 KB

-        57 MB

Step 3: The rëpartition of computerized data into organizational units and the consideration of data rights

Note here that we have the following workstations:

- The Head of Personnel ;

- The cashier accountant ;

- The head of the motor caravan.

NB: for the notations in the following diagrams, here are the meanings:

- C: right of consultation ;

- L: read right (record) ;

- M: right to modify ;

- S: right to delete.

Here are the MODs for each actor according to their attributions in the company:

For the Head of Personnel

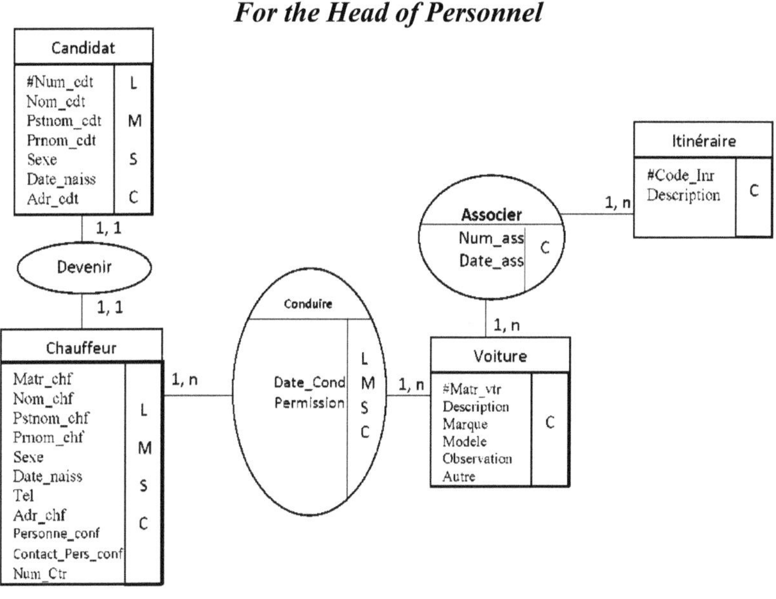

For the cash accountant :

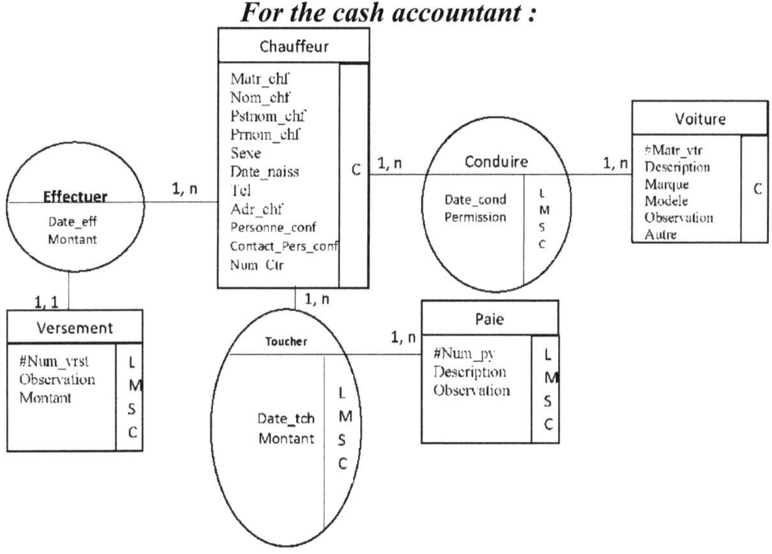

For the head of the motor caravan :

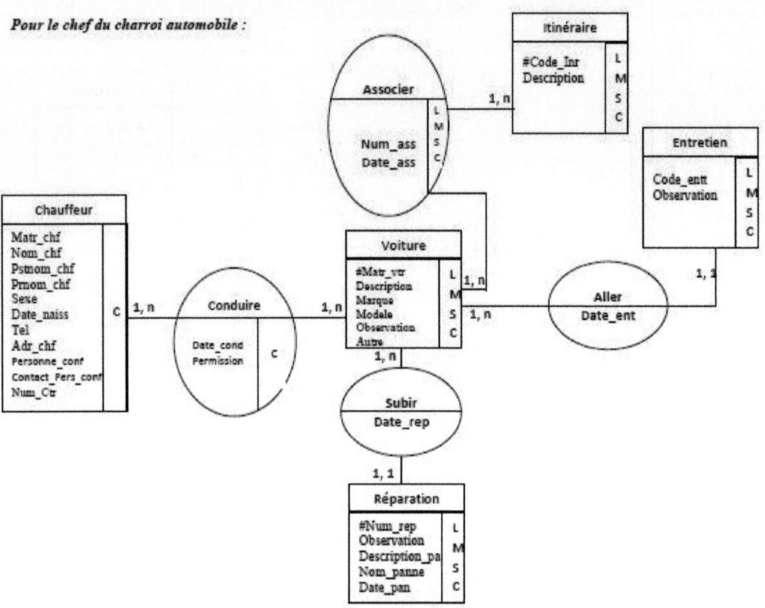

2. Setting up the logical data model

We now need to apply the rules for switching from MOD to raw MLD.

NB: for daughter-daughter relationships, according to common sense, we will force one of the parties to behave as a father to avoid having isolated tables (a table that is not related to any other table).

Here is the resulting raw MLD:

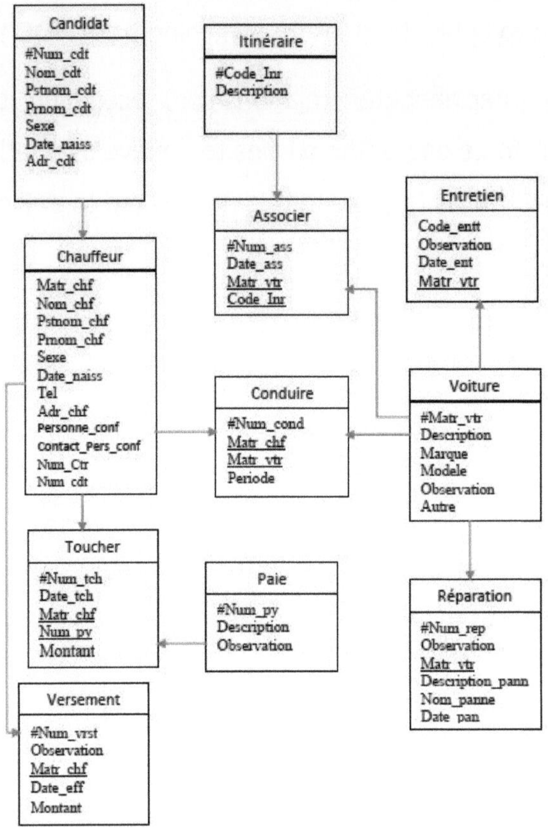

After analysing the raw LDM, we notice that, compared to the normalisation (taking into account the context in which we are and the needs of the users), precisely for the FN1 (principle of atomicity), all the attributes are atomic, except for the address of the candidate. With the address as in the raw LDM, we cannot analyse the proximity of the candidates to the workplace.

Hence this attribute must become a table that will give up its key to the candidate table.

Below is the valid MLD:

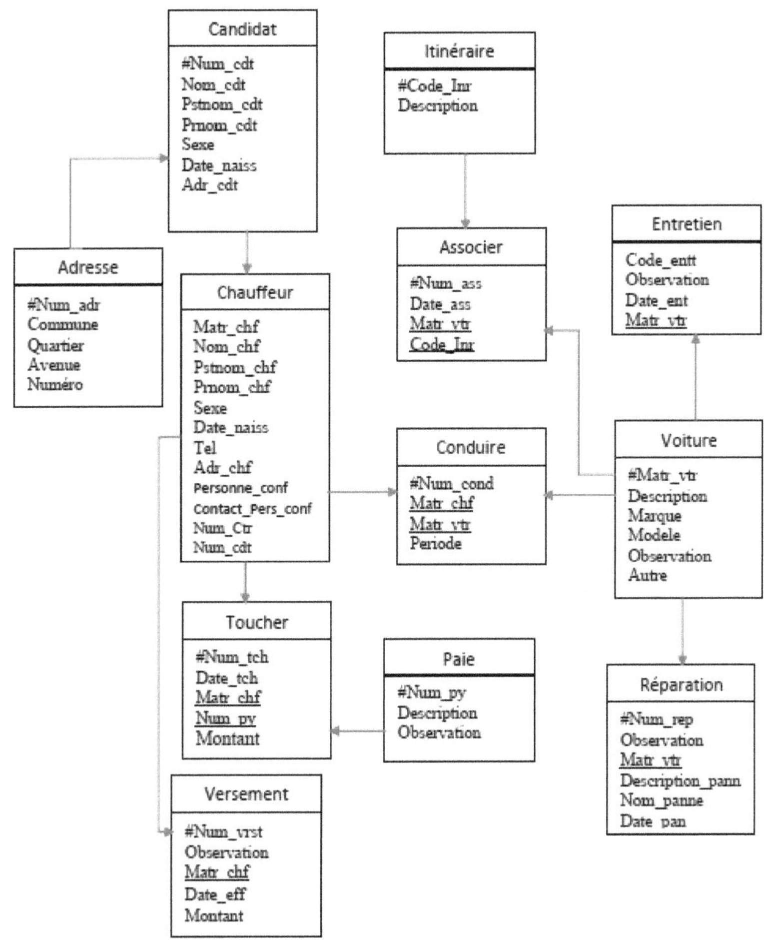

3) Physical level

The physical level constitutes the exit door of the merise method, it takes into account the concerns and technical choices necessary for the physical implementation of the data and the implementation of the treatments: programming language, choice of the DBMS, memory size...

a. Physical model of the data

In this problem, we have chosen SQL SERVER as the DBMS. We have the following model:

Create Database Gest_Trans;

Create table **Address** Num_adr int Primary key identity 1 1), Commune varchar(20) not null, Quartier varchar(30) not null, Avenue varchar(30) not null,Numero varchar(10) not null);

Create table **Candidate** Num_cdt int primary key identity(1 1 Nom_cdt varchar(20) not null, Pstnom_cdt varchar(20) not null, Prnom_cdt varchar 20 not null,Sexe char 1) not null CHECK(Sexe in('M','F')),Date_naiss date not null Adr_cdt int, foreign key Adr_cdt references Adresse ;

Create table **Driver** Matr_chf varchari6 primary key Nom_chf varchar(20) not null,Pstnom_chf varchar 20 not null,Prnom_chf varchar(20) not null,Sexe char 1) CHECK Sexe in('M','F')),Date_naiss date not null Tel varchar 14 default 'No number',Adr_chf varchar(40) not null,Personne_conf varchar 30) null,Contact_Pers_conf varchar(14) not null Num_Ctr int not null Num_cdt int, foreign key (Num_cdt references Candidate

Create table **Payroll** Num_py int primary key identity(1 1 Description_ varchar(30) not null,Observation varchar(50) default 'None');

Create table **Toucher** Num_tch int primary key identity 1 1 Date_tch date default Getdate(), Matr_chf varchar 6 Num_py int Amount decimal 6 2 not null, foreign key Matr_chf references Driver foreign key Num_py references Payroll);

Create table **Payment** Num_vrst int primary key identity 1 1),Observation varchar 40) default 'None'Matr_chf varchar(6 Date_eff date default Getdate(),Amount decimali6 2 not null, foreign key Matr_chf references Driver);

Create table **Itinerary** Code_Inr int primary key identity, 1 1 Description_ varchar(50) not null);

Create table **Car** Matr_vtr varchar 10 primary key,Description_ varchar(50) not null,Make varchar(25) not null,Observation varchar(50) default 'None',Other varchar(50) default 'None');

Create table **Associate** Num_ass int primary key identity, 1 1 Date_ass date not null,Matr_vtr varchar 10 Code_Inr int, foreign key i Matr_vtr references Car, foreign key (Code_Inr references Itinerary ;

Create table **Driving** Num_cond int primary key identity(1 1 Matr_chf varchar 6 Matr_vtr varchar, 10),Periode varchar 25) default 'Current',foreign key Matr_chf references Driver foreign key Matr_vtr references Car);

Create table **Maintenance** Code_entt int primary key identity 1 1),Observation varchar(50)   default 'None',Date_ent date default   Getdate() Matr_vtr varchar(10),foreign key i Matr_vtr references **Car**);

Create table **Repair** Num_rep int primary key identity 1 1),Observation varchar(50) default 'None',Matr_vtr varchar 10 Description_pann varchar 50) not null, Nom_panne varchar 35 not null Date_pan date default getdate(),foreign key Matr_vtr) references **Car** ;

CHAPTER 4

VERIFICATION OF RESPONSES TO USER NEEDS

41

The verification of end-user requirements is to ensure that all queries meeting these requirements return the expected results. We consider here only a representation of the queries for updating and for consultations.

- Need to manage all the drivers we recruit:
-        insert into Driver valuesCxxxxxx'/xxxxxx'/xxxxx'/M'/xxxx-xx- xx','+243xxxxxxxxxx','xxxxxxxx','xxxxxxxxx','xxxxxx',y,y);
-        update Driver set Matr_chf = 'xxxxx' where Matr_chf 'xxxxxx';
-        Delete from Driver where Matr_chf = '000243';
-        select * from Driver;

-      To analyse the proximity of a driver candidate's place of residence to the company's location, in order to avoid delays at work (assignment of the head of personnel).
-      select * from Applicant,Address where
(Candidate.Adr_cdt=Address.Num_adr)and(Address.Commune='XX X XX')and(Address.Quartier='YYYYY') order by Candidate.Nom_cdt;

-      To manage the payroll situation of the drivers, it should be noted that a driver is paid at the end of each month 12% of the total of his payments, the value of which is determined by the employer (allocation of the cashier).

-        insert into Payment Matr_chf Amount)values('xxxx' xx ;
-        insert into Payroll Description_ Observation values('xxxxxx','xxxxxxxx');
-        insert into Toucher Matr_chf Num_py Amount values('xxxxx' x xx ;

-        select * from Driver,Payroll,Touch where Driver Matr_chf Touch Matr_chf and(Payroll Num_py Touch Num_py) order by Driver Name_chf;

-        Of course, the UPDATE and DELETE commands are possible on these data.

- To manage the cars (each driver has a car at his disposal, no one else drives it in his absence, unless there is a special permission from the employer). Each car has a defined route (also changing the route is possible with special permission of the employer) (assignment of the head of the car transport).

```
-        insert into
Route Description_)values('xxxxxxxxxxxxx');
-        insert into Car
(Matr_vtr Description_ Brand Code_Inr Model)
values('xxxx','xxxx','xxxx',x,'xxxx');
-        insert into Conduire Matr_chf Matr_vtr
Periode)values ('xxxxxxxx', 'xxxxx', 'xxxxxxxxxx');
-        select * from Driver,Car,Driver where (Driver
Matr_chf = Driver Matr_chf) and Car Matr_vtr Driver
Matr_vtr);
```

-        Plan car maintenance (allocation of the head of personnel);
select * from Maintenance;

-        Identify recurring breakdowns for each make of vehicle to guide car maintenance (allocation by the Head of Personnel).
select distinct Panel_Name,Count Panel_Name from Repair group by Panel_Name

When there is a recruitment advertisement, the candidates each come and fill in an identification form where they fill in their identities. Then comes the recruitment test which determines whether a candidate is selected or not. When a candidate is selected, he completes his file by adding the contact details of at least one trusted person to be contacted in case of problems, before signing his contract which also gives information on the car that the new driver will drive in this company.

The driver will follow the route marked on his car every day, unless he has a special authorisation to go elsewhere, and will pay a fixed sum to the cashier at the end of each day. After a certain period of time (usually depending on the number of days the car is out), or in case of a breakdown, the car goes to the garage for maintenance or repair.

At the end of each month, a report must come from the cashier after the drivers' pay and another report must come from the garage on the maintenance and repairs carried out during the month.

CHAPTER 5

CRITICISM OF THE PROCEDURE

The clarity of the procedure leads us to say that with the MERISE method there are no flaws in the design of a database. The only challenge here is the accuracy of the totality of the needs of the end users of the database to be developed. Of course, other needs may arise over time, and modifying the database (its evolution) will only be easier if the company does not turn away from its initial objectives. Indeed, it will only be a matter of :

-       Adding an additional column to a table, or

-       The creation of a new table, which can only be related to an existing table in the database.

CONCLUSION

In this article we have tried to justify the choice of the MERISE method in the development of databases. We have systematically examined the approach proposed by MERISE through an application and have understood that it offers a very clear understanding of the IS. Redundancies and inconsistencies due to the invisibility of the approach are almost non-existent in the application of this procedure.

The problem with this approach is that a strong understanding of the end-users' needs is required before embarking on the design. This requires the designer to spend time in preliminary studies.

Furthermore, the low involvement of users in the design process is a disadvantage as it does not allow users to feel really concerned by the development of the database so that they adopt it easily.

As a future perspective, we recommend an agile version of MERISE which will allow to answer at first the visible needs and by iteration and incrementation to make evolve the database until covering all the needs of the company.

REFERENCES

1.   Bertrand LIAUDET, 'La methode MERISE", INSIA - SIGL 2.

2.   DI GALLO Frederic, " Methodologie de systeme d'information-MERISE ", CNAM ANGOULEME 2000-20010, unedited course.

3.   Musangu Luka, "Introduction a I'analyse informatique", EDUPC, Kinshasa, 2019.

4.   Nanci D., B. Espinasse with the collaboration of B. Cohen, J.C. Asselborn and H. Heckenroth (2001), "Ingenierie des systemes d'information : Merise deuxieme generation", Vuibert editions, Paris. ISBN: 2-7117-8674-9.

5.   Nicolas Moreau, "Expert opinion: Databases, a major challenge", IT Guide, 2017.

I want morebooks!

Buy your books fast and straightforward online - at one of world's fastest growing online book stores! Environmentally sound due to Print-on-Demand technologies.

Buy your books online at
www.morebooks.shop

Kaufen Sie Ihre Bücher schnell und unkompliziert online – auf einer der am schnellsten wachsenden Buchhandelsplattformen weltweit! Dank Print-On-Demand umwelt- und ressourcenschonend produzi ert.

Bücher schneller online kaufen
www.morebooks.shop

info@omniscriptum.com
www.omniscriptum.com

Printed by Books on Demand GmbH, Norderstedt / Germany